Where the Wild Blueberries Grow

Also by William Thornbro

In the Footsteps of Yeshua:
  An Ancient Guide to Living

The Coming of the Dryas:
  Amidst the Warming A Cold Weather Clock
  Ticks Away in the Northern Seas

An Uncertain Justice:
  Examination of the Eyewitness and Photographic
  Evidence in the Assassination of John F. Kennedy

Poems for Kids:
  For Childhood and Youth

A Midsummer's Dream:
  For Thought and Inspiration

The Would-be Adventures of Pub and Indy:
  A Discourse on the Public Mind

Where the Wild Blueberries Grow

Reflections of the Heart

A Collection of Poems by

William Thornbro

Artwork by *Judy Huff*

A Mayflower Center publication
www.mayflowercenterresearch.net
www.mcr.blue

To Dad,
William Wesley Elcannon Thornbro

Sometimes what is needed is a different way of looking at things. When you can wipe some of the color from your hands, the brush-strokes from your boots, climb over the frame, take a step back and get a look at the big picture.

Contents

For Kids, And Other Youngsters

Autumn Harvest

14

Introduction

The writing of a poem brings together every aspect of being. It is your every degree of mind and spirit; it is all of your love, your compassion; it is every bit of your knowing- your everything is brought to the task. This is a book of poems for a purpose; to inspire, to encourage, to motivate and even to educate- and for all ages, including childhood and youth. For me, when I am at my best, it is often an attempt- as in the poem, *On This Day of Days*- to capture a solitary moment; to preserve for all time a thought, an idea, a conviction- an image of a single day. This work is a complete collection of my poems- so far. It is an auto-biographical work of sorts, I am going to say, for it embraces a lot of long-held hopes and dreams- reflections on a life lived. A few words of wisdom, perhaps- there is a bit of philosophical content; mixed in, I suppose, with some of the inevitable stumbling and foolishness of a lifetime, and topped off with a little verse and rhyme. Most of the poems will be found to be accompanied by an image, which can provide a useful focal-point for the thoughts and images that may arise in the mind in their reading. All are original art; a benefit of having a sister who is an artist. This is the first publication for most of this work, aside from 14 poems that are published under the title, *A Midsummer's Dream*, 2013. A portion of it, mostly those poems listed in the section for children, is published separately and concurrently in a volume entitled, *Poems for Kids*. This book's title is from a poem about my father, to whom it is dedicated; for his caring, his sweat and toil, his hugs- his laughing eyes, and cheek-to-cheek grin. I consider this to be my signature work; here-in lie my thoughts, my heart and my soul- welcome to my world! And so it is with the greatest pleasure that I now present to you, *Where the Wild Blueberries Grow*.

Wm Thornbro- April, 2021

To stand at the very summit that words can reach; to touch the beauty, the wisdom, and the stillness, that lies beyond.

At the Summit

When light and shadow, and gentle wind, come to run and play.

Among Green Leaves

Out among the green leaves in the garden;
On the wings of their every turn in the wind;
And in their shadowy and elusive reflections,
That play upon my wall in the late afternoon.

An ode to every tree, every leaf and leaflet;
To a thousand Summers that have yet to come;
To a thousand Springs that have already been;
A song to every flower, every petal, every bloom.

As the Sun comes to light the performance,
Their every motion a geometry extraordinaire.
A new thought arises, an insight never known;
The words of a stoic- an old forgotten tune.

In Nature's long, unfolding and untold story,
I come to this one single page, again and again.
In the quiet of my room, and out in the garden;
Woven into the fabric on Heaven's great loom.

Never let the mere facts of a matter get in the way of truth. As a nested bird one day raises itself up and finds its wings, a truth begins a fact and then which has learned how to fly.

A Place Within

Always keep a place in your mind where you can go;
Where you can contemplate what is close to your heart.
This will be for you a place of the greatest comfort;
Words, teachings, thoughts, memories, will guide you.

Your experience may be a quiet and solitary meditation;
It may be a poem, or it may be a simple happy tune.
Or it can be of words, or of some symbols or imagery,
Far beyond the bounds of the usual understanding.

This is a place where you can see yourself most clearly;
It's about hopes and dreams- of divine and noble truths.
It is a place without limit-of unbound enlightenment;
It is to see the world from the highest point of view.

And it is from here that you can see your way forward,
Whether on the brightest of days, or the darkest night.
May your experience be for you a perception wider,
An insight deeper, than anything that you have known.

May each and every hope and dream become a signpost,
Along your path to a full and truly lasting happiness.
May you find for yourself some purpose- a real meaning;
And in the midst of it all, a great peace in your life.

May that light which has inspired and sustained the hearts of others, that has shown the way for those who have come before, now illuminate you and me!

The Treasure

At the end of the earth, and the end of the day;
When the Sun sweeps its colors in its final display;
There's a peace and serenity that time will not find;
And I its lone witness- come to dream and untwine.

My mind here can play, and my soul take a rest;
Where a thought inmost becomes the out-most best.
And with a rhythm and grace only the sea can keep,
Waves scatter the shore with its wonders deep.

I can see it now before me in the glistening sand;
All the world's reflection in the palm of my hand.
What I once held followed the Sun into the sea,
Is right here, and all around, and illuminates me.

Oh that I could stay in the magic of this place!
The cares of the day a new hope doth replace.
But the shadows lengthen, and I return to the town;
To tell my story, to share the treasure that I found.

What are words but an humble representation of the rich and subtle array of imagery that color our dreams, that play along the pathway of the mind.

To the Iris in Spring

Gone the baron frozen stream;
The Sun has lift its solemn veil.
Where was the Winter wind,
New life and Spring prevail.

Hope reborn, a world made new;
Terra restored her rightful place;
To which you bring, O' flower,
A relevance certain, and grace.

Now I believe in miracles;
In a Winter's dream come true.
For truly, the promise of Spring,
Is here in this moment with you.

Filled with your breath,
It's a day for heart and mind;
For in the depths of your being,
A joy in my own I find.

"The work of a good man is like an underground stream- secretly making the grass greener" -Thomas Carlyle.

A Midsummer's Dream

My search for the old poet's wellspring,
Leads ever to the shade of a solitary tree.
On a hillside green, in the quiet pasture lane;
The history it has seen is compelling to me.

Here is the promise of a midsummer's dream.
What opens the heart will fill the gentle soul;
Begins an illumination- a thought of the mind;
As at the end of a stream, a river does flow.

I hang on the words, breathe in their meaning;
They're not just the same- the mist and the rain;
And a road less traveled, a difference makes;
A voice clear and true as the robin's oft refrain.

Deep in my dream the tree's contour I trace;
An ancient wisdom I endeavor to discern.
Like its rings, a mystery comes full circle;
A river in its time to its source will return.

A lot of the best ideas tend to arrive completely unexpected, in a wrapping totally unfamiliar, and from a sender unknown.

The Rain

In the sights and sounds of a rainy day,
The poet is often not content;
But is beckoned to go out and stand in it.
Our best hopes and dreams,
Are such that words alone can not reach them;
That which only verse can begin to describe.

The imagination soars, the heart weeps- it sings!
A divine inspiration stirs at the soul.
An illumination, fleeting, seemingly ephemeral,
Guides the pen to capture on paper,
What the heart longs to say;
What is it like- the mist against the face?

"I have brought you to the ring, now dance the best you can"
- William Wallace

A Knight's Code

Stand now before the alter of your very soul;
That flame eternal which lives deep within.
Fall upon your knees, receive your blessing;
That your heart will know only virtue;
That your words speak only for truth.
In the words of Jefferson before you,
Swear a mighty oath against tyranny;
Against all forms of evil over man.
Your words will be your great armor;
Your deeds are your shinning sword.
Arise and live your guiding principles;
Let them be emblazoned upon your heart.
Summon the courage to live, and to love;
You are the one already you would become.

Gently In Your Thoughts

When you experience beauty,
When you experience stillness,
It is of the most precious of things.
It is in your most solemn moments,
And it is in the deepest of your dreams.

It is in tune with the birds,
In their early morning song;
It is the wind in fields of golden grain;
It is the late day Sun in leaves of green,
And the watery ripple on a moonlit pond.

It is the subtle and fleeting scent,
that, in an instant, returns you,
To a day you thought long since past.
It is a glance, a breath, a touch;
It is love's embrace- a hug from a friend.

Like an ever-flowing stream,
It is steady and all-pervading;
It touches everyone and everything;
It is everywhere and also every-when;
Its pulse is the rhythm of every single mind.

Such an experience is not to be possessed,
And it need not be defined.
Just hold it gently in your thoughts;
Enjoy it- be with it in the moment;
It will lighten the day's toil and burden.

And, like the little butterfly,
Its impression will be forever in your heart.

To the Sons of Adam /To the Daughters of Eve

Be true to yourself, be true to your purpose, and be true to others; and what you seek in the great round of life, yourself, you will find. What you do and say, and also what you think and feel, will have profound meaning in your life- always.

Follow your own dreams. Never allow others, no matter how much you love them, to define who you are; this important task you must reserve for yourself. In terms of your essential self, of who you really are, you don't need to make any changes; you don't need to be anyone or anything other than who you already are. You are whole and you are complete, and you have been so all along- since the beginning.

Do what you can to heal the hurts of others, but their ill words and deeds are not yours; do not accept their guilt as yours, do not take on their suffering as your own. When you come to see the ego and its pain in others, you won't feel the need to keep it, or to pass it on- you can instead just let it go away.

As much as you can, fill your life with happiness. Calm the noisy restless stream of thoughts and feelings that rush across your mind. You may have thought it was you solving problems, but it isn't; its mostly bits and pieces of past hurts, and mindless chatter. See it for what it is, and allow it to go away. Replace it with a hope or a dream, a poem, or a happy tune. It's what you're thinking that largely determines your day.

Listen to and sooth your inner child; that part of you that retains the hurt inflicted by others. Learn forgiveness; free yourself from the suffering of the past, and tomorrow's fears; there's plenty of room for you right here in the present. If you insist on having to worry, then at least make it about something over which you have some say. To the extent that your concern is in the control of someone else, worry will tend to bring you sorrow.

Worship your heroes and honor your best teachers; take what they offer and make it your own. But you need not idealize words and teachings; there will always be other words to express your meaning, and other teachings that will guide you to the same place.

Look within your heart for peace, and for meaning. There are many things to learn that will help you along life's way; and may you find another who will bring you much happiness; a spouse, a child, a soul-mate, or a best friend. But if you are to know true peace, and if you are to find purpose in your life, this is not something another can give- you will not find yourself in another. The peace of life and its meaning is only to be found by you, and it is only to be found within. This is where it will always be, and this is where it has always been.

It's the journey that matters; life is not a mere means to an end. Don't worry about an exact destination, just set a general course and begin. When things don't seem quite right, consult your inner compass- you'll want to make some changes along the way. And your journey's end will be like a sweet ripe fruit that awaits you at the end of the day.

Do not be discouraged! Know that you are loved by others, and by those who have come before. In the great and limitless Cosmos, in the great scheme of things, you are truly the child of the Earth and of Heaven; as much and the same as skies and stars.

Out From the Poverty of Suffering

I would like to speak to you now about finding yourself; it is the overcoming of a poverty of the spirit that has pervaded all of humanity since the very beginning. If you are successful you will find yourself among an elect group; it is something which I suspect relatively few have ever achieved. Finding yourself is at the very heart of an ancient guide to living, consisting of teachings of Jesus- they are his own words. I'm referring to a document called The Gospel of Thomas, found in the Egyptian desert in 1945. I cannot over-emphasis the importance of this one single thing; it is the best thing you will ever do for yourself. Find yourself and you will find out what it is in which you truly believe- you will find your faith. Find yourself and you will find your life- you will know what it is to truly live. You will have learned the way out of suffering, and I cannot find the words to adequately express the importance of what this means. The pathway toward accomplishing this great goal is simply to go within, and to help you get started, the next few paragraphs, in particular, are intended as a kind of meditation that you may want to utilize; perhaps until you have come up with something that is more your own. It is very much like one I have used for myself; and I have indented some lines that I would like you to read as your own words to yourself.

While our speaking of consciousness and the inner mind as separate things is not necessarily reflective their true nature, it does provide a means by which we may think and discuss aspects of mind, of our thoughts, that we find difficult to approach by any means. We can, therefore, see the mind within as that part of ourselves that pays attention to everything; and especially when consciousness has a something important to say. On some regular basis, find yourself some alone-time; some time to spend with just you. Relax and calm the thoughts of the day; clear the mind- turn your thoughts inward. Your interactions with others invariably accumulates some suffering, some guilt, some pain, and which needs your attention; bring your thoughts to it, recognize it, and let it go. That is not to say that I think there is some sort of concerted effort on the part of others to cause suffering in you, or necessarily to anyone. Much of it I think is unconscious; that people do regularly cause this kind of grief for friends, family, and others, and, most of the time, without ever being aware of it. It can be seen as a kind of collective ego that, unfortunately, pervades the whole of humanity. This suffering is transferred from person to person in the course of our daily interactions with one another; it moves easily within families, and we tend to pass it on to our children.

Everyone is affected to some extent by this seemingly mass insanity, with the weaker, and meeker, of us being most affected; it is especially true of those of us who are most impressionable, such as young children. I understand this as a need by everyone to find relief from their own acquired suffering; the guilt and pain they have accepted from others. That suffering that you experience was first that of someone else, it did not begin with you- and in that sense it is not truly yours. It was a long time before I understood this, and I hope will not be so long a time for you.

Do not seek to drop your own burden of suffering into the laps of others; do not add to the burdens others already carry. It is not for us to try to convert anyone to our own beliefs, nor should we want to define them, or to place them in a particular role that they must play. These things are for others to figure out for themselves. Love them for who they are; they need not make any changes to their true selves, and we can only hope that others will afford us the same.

Utilize the power of meditation- of trance- and affirmations. This whole writing is really an affirmation; write something out for yourself- something that is just for you. This is something to keep with you; to re-write when you feel the need, or just read whenever you need a reminder. Make it your own- your own personal truth. It is important to know that reviewing your affirmations, meditating on or re-reading your own words, and especially the physical act of writing them down, has a powerful influence with the mind, that part of us that is the source of intelligence and creativity. Do this on a regular basis; this is something that you will not grow tired of:

I relax and go within. I release all of the suffering, the guilt and pain from the past, that which I have accepted from others, that has been caused by others. I release with ease all of the physical tension and emotional pain, all of the old worn out beliefs and fears; I observe them and then I let them go. Once they are recognized for what they are they disappear, they fade and they are gone. I Forgive those who have caused harm toward me, not so much because they are necessarily deserving of forgiveness, but to forgive myself for internalizing and retaining the guilt from their actions or their words. My own act of forgiveness allows me the freedom to move on. I am not to blame for the hurt inflicted by others, whether the victim was myself, or someone else. Indeed, I am sorry for them, for the unconscious and unnecessary burden that they bear; but they no longer have any power over me- I am the captain of my own ship.

There is a tendency for the victim to identify with the one who has caused his/her suffering, and to bring that same suffering to others. It is, for example, the wife who accepts the abuse of an angry husband, and takes her frustrations out on others; it is the child who has been told by parents, and other often well-meaning people that there is something wrong with him/her, and who grows up to inflict those same beliefs on others, and on their own children. So you will also need to forgive yourself for the suffering you have brought to others, because we have all done so:

I am now willing to free myself from the past- I do not live there anymore. I now have a new understanding of who I am, and who I am not. My name is not me, and neither is my body within which I live. Both are gifts from my parents, and both are a kind of label who others recognize, but they say nothing of my essential self. I am not a collection of my past experiences, nor am I my thoughts; my thoughts are mine, and my experiences are determined at least partly by me, but they are not me. Neither am I who others may want me to be, or expect me to be; as much as I may love them, I will not- do not- allow others to define who I am. This important task I reserve for myself. So, exactly who am I? I am the spirit, the soul; I am the awareness of things, and beyond this I do not feel a need to be defined. I am whole and I am complete, and my sense is that I have been so all along- since the beginning. I may make changes from time to time in things that are about me, but in terms of my essential self, there is no need for me to be anything other than who I already am.

To know this is to know in the very highest sense that you have become free to be you. An ego driven mania has dominated the headlines of human history for far too long. It is time to stop bringing suffering to the world; and it is time to stop bringing it within ourselves. We have it within us to achieve never before known heights; for each of us an awareness of spirit, and for all of humanity a new way of being. It is, in a spiritual sense, time to evolve!

To the extent that we see others as somehow less than ourselves; that is illusion, and it is a measure of our suffering. To the extent that we see ourselves as more deserving than others; that too is illusion, and a measure of our suffering. We may think that we know more than others, and in some instances that may be true, but all of our heady thoughts of being somehow better are illusory- and they are a measure of our suffering.

Finding yourself importantly involves the unconditional acceptance of yourself; it is the belief that you, in your true self, are OK, just as you are- that you don't need to make any of those kinds of changes. Give the time necessary with these thoughts to allow them to find their way in; you will need to think them through on your own- write them down. On any given day your prospects for obtaining awareness improves; on any given day the fire burns a little brighter; a little more light shines into the darkness; a new thought becomes known- another connection is made.

An excerpt from, *In the Footsteps of Yeshua*, 2018

'The one who has found and knows her soul has found all the world'
- ancient Indian Upanishad.

Every Rock and Wellspring

We find ourselves on this day, you and I,
Stewards of a great and very ancient land.
The sons and daughters in an age-old story;
Far older than anything ever written down.

Many are those who have come before us,
And whose many sacrifices we honor today.
Ours is a story of toil, and much suffering,
But a story too of much hope and much love.

The trees of the earth, the birds of the sky;
Each and every rock and every wellspring;
They too are a part of that same old story;
All images, all reflections, of a greater reality.

Our best thoughts, our reverence for spirit,
Every blessing, every prayer and meditation;
All expressions of that great soul that is within;
All at the last the manifestation of the divine.

The lighting of a candle, a loved fragrance,
Cherished words from an old favorite song;
Each with their own bit of spiritual wisdom;
All from the same great experience of being.

On a Little Golden Pond

A great star heralds the dawn,
Amidst the slumbering shadows of night.
The old lion of the Nile is its witness;
In the early mist, in the morning light.

Small as the waking butterfly,
And as much as the sky beyond;
In a land and valley most ancient;
And here, on a little golden pond.

A tiny droplet rests on a leaflet;
Its time in the Sun now here;
Softly it glistens in the twilight;
Its wide and perfect circle draws near.

Look deeply into this moment;
Things afar off are here within.
All comes together in the stillness;
All that will be, and all that has been.

In the simplest and smallest of things,
As in the greatest and grandest of things,
There is the reflection of all things.
Ananda, open your sleepy eyes!

As the rain gives way to sunshine;
As the summer will turn to fall;
As on Earth, so it is in Heaven;
The key to one is the key to all.

A tiny droplet rests on a leaflet;
A butterfly readies its wings for flight.
One glorious and eternal moment,
In the stillness of the morning light.

When relationships with others are right, everything matters; it is in fact only then that anything does.

Where the Wild Blueberries Grow

I'll tell you a little story,
About a place that I know;
Its up in the far meadow,
Where the wild blueberries grow.

How my dad one time stood,
Where the best of them now aspire;
Where before was a shaded wood,
That had been taken in a fire.

With laughter in his eyes,
And his cheek-to-cheek grin,
He planted and he worked and cared,
To bring the place to life again.

In the burned and baron ground,
He saw a rich and fertile soil;
And in a little wide-eyed child,
A new hope for his sweet and toil.

Wisdom of the Heart

It's our thinking that gets us by,
In our busy lives from day-to-day;
But on a question of the heart,
It's the heart that must have say.

Its words may be but a few,
And only once may they be heard;
So Listen, and listen very carefully,
And hear its every single word.

When the day is filled with sorrow,
And thoughts are doom and gloom;
Such are gone in just a moment,
When heart comes in the room.

When your life is at a crossroads,
Old things can be made anew;
When heart brings out its wisdom,
A perfect attention to it is due.

Heart is a life changing moment,
When a great foundation is laid;
The place of strength and wisdom,
When big decisions must be made.

For all the rest of your days,
On such days will life depend;
Thought left to decide alone,
Is a fate left to wayward wind.

Wanting is not just like needing,
And both in a moment may be gone;
Neither says very much of love true,
Which asks nothing of either one.

And when love has made its calling,
And your feet can't touch the floor;
When thought has lost all its senses,
Heart is still with you- and evermore.

The trees will all be green again,
And once again the sky made blue;
Heaven and Earth is made new again,
When again the heart shows true.

Sun and Moon their homage pay;
The day is brighter than before;
When heart comes to step in again,
Miracles happen, hope's in store.

Love is great, but can be blind;
And thought all alone cannot fly;
Both may know what day it is,
But only heart can tell you why

Indiana Woods

I find the woods in Autumn an enchanting place to be.
I love the many colored leaves;
The fragrance, the sounds of the trees;
And the stillness, when it's there.

The pilgrim's singular quest imparts a vision which opens many doors; the path of wisdom leads to all places.

New Hope

As old Winter days begin to lengthen;
As the day begins to catch up to the night;
When the last snow has fled from the land,
And there is the coming of a new Spring;
A new day is dawn- a new day of light.

It may be that the only true claim that any of us have to wisdom is in knowing that in the course of our lives we are all sometimes the fool. What is wisdom anyway but the finally having gained some benefit from an accumulation of years of foolishness.

Soul-Awareness

Not galaxies, nebula, their planets and stars;
It is life, it is life itself, that is truly enduring.
And deep within each of us- every one of us,
Does a single drop of its precious essence reside.

Within the bounds of the world that we know,
It cannot be contained, nor can it be defined.
We are the reflection of a far greater reality;
To that perfect soul is our awareness our bond.

"To know that even one other life has breathed because you lived, this is to
have succeeded" - Ralph Waldo Emerson

There can be no greater honor, no greater significance, than this.

A Father's Love

We have walked together now on many paths;
On many paths did I travel before I knew you;
And you too, will go some ways that I have not;
A day will come when you will go on without me.

I have made for you, in my heart, a special place;
As much as any, do I long to see your smiling face;
As much as Sun, Moon, flowers and trees- I confess,
My love for you is just as much and never less.

Whatever you do, no matter the path you will take,
Know that whenever it is that you have need of me,
Whenever the day brings you some thought of me,
That I am with you- and so will I be with you always.

My soul loves to walk its wooded deep, as the Sun drifts slowly away to sleep.

For the Love of Trees

Come along and I'll show you a secret treasure;
It's in a wooded sanctuary along the ole town way.
You can hear, when it's there, its earthy stillness;
And learn the words to what the sparrows say.

Long forgot days of Sun can still be found there;
And Fall's windswept golds and browns and reds.
On a Winter's evening you can walk and wonder;
The woods filled with soft white blankets in its beds.

And nestled in among heaps of late Winter leaves,
Everywhere! An explosion of life is about to begin.
And next season's dying too, when it comes around,
Is still of the same great experience life has been.

Oh, I think it is the love of trees that beckons me,
And it's the rocky path that winds through between.
So many hopes and so many dreams have found me,
Where the ole log rests o'er little bubbling stream.

In the woods I can watch the mist as it slowly rises;
The squirrel, when I forget, shows me how to play.
Clear skies or no, I leave the town far behind me;
And the bonds of illusion simply fall, and fall away.

Not in every season does the life-stream of the wooded maple flow; sweet inspiration, that hallowed and treasured moment, will come in its own time, and of it's own accord.

Of Light and Shadow

In a land of enchantment, in an Autumn field of trees;
Deep and deep in reflection, and the scent of fallen leaves.
Warmed and cradled in the soft glow of a yellow Sun;
Already old in days when the days of man were young.

Here is a presence that I nowhere else have known;
As by chance or by magic the trees are spirits their own.
My mind moves among them, above time and above place;
Whispers of eternity fill the wood, and my own inner space.

Here Nature weaves her tapestry in a most wondrous display,
When light and shadow, and gentle wind, come to run and play.
A sacred sign, an ancient word, subtle imagery abound;
In the trees overhead, and their fleeting silhouettes all around.

I walk her wanton path, her way of crimsons, her golds sublime;
Past and future melt into present, into song and into rhyme.
I am become the child, I am as the wind, a blue and endless sky;
A stillness settles within, moves deeper, shall never die.

Her quiet word, her breath, only deepens the trance;
In the leaves, her secrets, a light and shadow fairie dance.
The wind moves, a leaf is turned, Nature shows her hand;
I lay my head and dream a dream of something new in the land.

Every thought that will ever be is here, in a single afternoon;
Every heart that ever was, still true, as the light of the Moon.
Such a shining moment, what wings the mind does tend;
A great harvest for the soul at the Summer season's end.

Above wanting, birth and death, is a higher calling; it is our awareness that gives what we know meaning;

Its Wooded Deep, Its Starry Shore

I'm often chided for the time that I take,
Wandering as I do along woods and lake.
When the Sun and wind run in the trees,
I want to jump and to play in the breeze.

When morning's colors light up the sky,
I want a front row seat, right here nearby.
When the lake whispers its lovely song,
I want to be here- I want to sing along.

My soul loves to walk its wooded deep,
As the Sun drifts slowly away to sleep.
And the evening's twilight evermore,
Will find my heart along its starry shore.

When tomorrow asks about this place,
Away as it is from the hurry and race;
My words and rhyme have taken shape,
Here in the woods and along the lake.

Every blessing, every prayer and meditation; all expressions of that great soul that is within.

The Shepherd's Lonely Song

We lie in the lap of a greater reality- of immense heaven;
Beyond the world that we know there is, Oh, so much more!
Barely discernible within the bounds of conscious thinking,
It was here before death and before any of us were born.

Yet when my mind is subtle I can touch it with my thought;
In its divine presence I have been many times in a dream.
I know its warmth, I know its embrace, its comfort, its calm;
Its still water soothes my face, soothes my hands and my feet.

I am as the child, my awareness emanates from this source;
All pervasive and yet formless, perceived and yet unseen;
It is what the ear will hear, and it is what the eye will see,
And that which has never before fallen upon the tongue.

It is here, it is in the life-breath, and it is in the stars of night;
It is in an ancient psalm, it is in the shepherd's lonely song;
It is a great light in the darkness, it is the heart set on flame;
Guard it until it blazes, for it is enough to light the world.

All things great and small, all those days gone by and all those yet to be, have their reflection in the present moment.

Reflections of Eternity

We are babes in the arms of an immense and eternal wisdom. It is spread out across the land; it is in the sea; it finds its expression in you- it finds its expression in me.

It is the great celestial event within which we find ourselves; it is that vast cosmic tapestry against which we each pursue our singular journeys here on this Earth.

It is in the starry sky, it is in every mortal breath; it is in everything that there is, and yet we can hardly touch it with our thought.

It is what the eye will see; it is what the ear will hear; it is all that is beyond the physical world, the world that we know, and it is woven everywhere within it.

It has been since the very beginning, long before any of us were born. A universal symphony, of which we may have had by chance a mere glimpse of a few notes.

It is a great congregation of souls; it is the great power and wealth from which each of us have come, and to which we each, in our time, will return.

It is all that will be, and it is all that has been; it is here in this present moment; it is all of this, and it is everything.

A little flower growing at the edge of the garden basks in the Sun; it reaches into the soil- soaks up its nutrients and the rain. It is happy with itself; it wants for no other place, it seeks no position- it wants no power over other flowers. It lives today, in and of itself, and in this moment- and it is this moment!

When Heaven Looks This Way

For far too long has war defined this humanity;
For far too long has conflict been the headlines.
When other ways and means of theft have failed,
A war is for the taking of other people's lands.

It is only power and wealth that gains anything;
For everyone else it brings on suffering and death.
It is the true evil that pervades all of our history;
It is a great poverty that mankind itself has made.

Wars and more wars- the true scourge of mankind;
It is not the lilies of the field that take what is yours.
It makes you wonder if we are really all that worthy,
Of the top place we hold in the life here on Earth.

When the time comes that Heaven looks this way,
Is it a planet in conflict that we want to be seen?
With daughter against mother, father against son;
It's time to grow up; to evolve- don't you think?

Five Things to Do

1 Be the seeker
2 Find yourself
3 Find your faith
4 Take your place
5 Light a lamp for others

I have often found, at the end of the day, about a thing acquired, that its wanting was not the least thing.

That one lives within which the spirit thrives.

Top Ten Goals for the New Century

1. To provide everyone clean water; to feed the hungry
2. To provide shelter for the homeless; to clothe those in need
3. To care for and to educate our children
4. To care for the elderly; it is they who cared for us
5. To learn to care for ourselves
6. To Learn to live with a changing climate
7. To finally put an end to all war
8. To bring everyone- all people- together, into the human fold
9. To finally begin to live out the true meaning of our creed
10. To put an end to suffering, everywhere and whenever we can

Hints: They're pretty much the same goals as for all the previous centuries; succeed with #10 and you will have done what you can with 1 through 9.

March of the Rose

Come, let us march to the drums of the heroes;
May their words now echo throughout the land.
Let us march to where they lay in eternal rest;
To the places stained with their hallowed blood.

Let us now carry the rose proudly before us,
As the symbol of the great sacrifice they made;
To all the statehouses and to the courthouses;
To the places of power, and the places of wealth.

'Let us dream of those things that never were,
And say to the world, why haven't they been;' [1]
'That all men and all women are created equal;' [2]
Free in our own homes, and upon our own lands.

'May we swear a mighty oath against tyranny;' [3]
Privilege for the few comes at too high a cost;
Not slaves, but free to be about our own work;
The woman in the street- the man on the farm.

"Be not afraid;" for we are brave- we're strong; [4]
'There's nothing to fear, except just our fear;' [5]
Let tyranny and injustice now be vanquished;
Let them answer for the wrongs they've made.

For the generations that have come before us;
Their years of toil- their blood, sweat and tears;
To their voices against evil may we add our own;
On that same field of valor let us take our stand.

Arm-in-arm with our brothers and our sisters;
On shoulders of giants, 'we come to the ring;' [6]
We are determined and we are great in number;
Now is our time- 'let us dance as best we can.' [7]

'We're all mortal- we all breathe the same air;' [8]
'And we all cherish the futures of our children;' [9]
'Let us live out the true meaning of our creed;' [10]
'Captains of our souls- the masters of our fate.' [11]

Arise and live your guiding principles; let them be emblazoned upon your heart.

[1] Robert Kennedy; [2 & 3] Thomas Jefferson; [4] Mohandas Gandhi;
[5] Franklin Roosevelt ; [6 & 7] William Wallace; [8 & 9] John Kennedy;
[10] Martin King; [11] Nelson Mandela, (quoting William Henley).

Realizing that each and every life has its own enduring purpose, enjoy your life; learn to love, to help others- do some good things.

Its Expression My Hand

How I long for its understanding,
Yet I know not whence it came.
My heart is filled with its message,
And yet I know it not by name.

It is that sweet and loved melody,
That carries along as the wind.
That solemn and revered silence,
That follows a prayer that we send.

It is as the great strength of a lion;
The gentle voice that is the lamb;
An immense and eternal wisdom;
And I its word- its expression I am.

Life is truly a great and wonderful experience, with the one possible exception of when you don't think so. Think about what is possible; love others- believe in yourself.

On This Day of Days

As I walk among the trees now in mid-October,
And seek a favorite bench along a rocky stream,
The leaves are brown and red, and golden-yellow;
Gone are their Summer's many shades of green.

Aimlessly they chase one another downward,
Frolicking in the air with all their fellow leaves.
On the ground the race only gets faster and faster;
Running with not a care, playing in the breeze.

My heart wants to stay here all day in the woods;
My soul whispers some words to a favorite song.
Its such an invitation I cannot very long resist;
Soon we're all wandering off and singing along.

Oh that I might capture this one single moment;
That I may save for all time a lucid image of this day.
May that I can dwell upon its every drop of sunlight,
When even the pale Winter has come to hold sway.

Who would have thought that today of all days;
A day just like any other when the day began;
That today would bring such fun, such sweetness;
For I have found myself in the woods once again.

For Kids, and Other Youngsters

Spring magic

It's Spring!

When gray skies have departed,
And the snow has all melted away;
When red robin begins to sing again,
And the Sun again warms up the day.

It's time to put some play clothes on;
Hats and coats are in the closet to stay.
The swing and the bike are calling;
It's time to run and to jump and play.

Joy of Winter

What's Special About Being a Kid?

A kid's sense of wonder is worth holding on to;
The smell of a little flower in a meadow of flowers;
The wind in the trees, and across fields of grain;
And the touch of winter's frost on a window glass.

Always remember the joy, the lightness, of being you;
Think of the openness- your acceptance of other kids;
Remember when another kid gave these things to you;
Always love others, and others will always love you.

A kid should not have to worry about grown-up things;
It's to love and be loved- it's about the simple things.
You must find yourself- you must find out who you are;
Growing up will be fun if you hold on to all of these.

We'll sail to the Sun!

To the Sun

We'll sail to the Sun while the Sun is still shinning;
And when the day is done, and the evening comes,
In the high glen we'll build us a great and roaring fire.
We'll feast, we'll tell stories, we'll sing and we'll rest,
Till the morning comes, and we'll hoist our sails again.

Little Annie May

Today Little Annie May walked to the candy store;
Every color and flavor from the ceiling to floor.
Which of these delicious treats will be hers today?
Which one will she choose to take out the door?
Oh, the rest will be there for her on another day;
For sure, on another day, she will be back for more.

I believe!

Snowflakes and Flowers

I believe in snowflakes,
And in a warm sunny day.
I love when Autumn comes,
And all the flowers in May.

The BFFL

Love is in all people, in those faces of caring all around;
It is in the look of approval between a parent and a child;
It is those sweetest of moments, and in life's many norms.

It is for that life-long soul mate, the BFFL, the best friend;
A gift that arrives the next time around in a new wrapping,
Love comes in many shapes and sizes, and in many forms.

To everything a time

Minutes and Hours/ Hours and Days

Life is made of many little moments;
There are plenty of minutes and hours,
And lots of room and time for play.

Minutes make hours, hours make days;
And it is up to us to make use of them;
To catch them before they get away.

Let it Fall Like the Rain

Let those harsh words of critics,
Fall away like the summer rain.

Not feeling good about oneself,
Can make one angry and vain.

The ill words and deeds of others,
Are but the face of their pain.

Happy to be

At Home By the Sea

Long did I dream there's better places to be;
Something was missing in my life by the sea.
With no treasures down there for me left behind,
I climbed up the mountain to see what I'd find.

I'd longed for some newness, to be out and be free;
Over the mountain is where I thought I should be.
So I climbed to the top and saw a big rolling plain;
But except for the sea it looked a lot just the same.

Oh, I left a great burden on the mountain that day;
Some fear and expectation was at last gone away.
At home by the sea I'm now quite happy to be;
And now I know really what it's like to be free.

Heaven's work is our work

Heaven's Work

As the shopkeeper counts his wares,
As the magistrate declares his say,
Who will care for the children?
Who will comfort the sick, the old?

As the town crier calls the time to us,
As the woodsman cuts and cuts away,
Who will feed those who hunger?
And the one left out in the cold?

It is we who live in this moment;
It is up to us at the end of the day.
Heaven's work is surely our own;
Love is greater than silver and gold.

Do you see it? Orange skies!

Where Do Things Come From?

Mother, Where does a song come from?

Well, it begins as a tune someone thinks up;
What do you hear?

How about a painting, where do you start?

It starts out an image in one person's mind;
What do you see?

Father, Where do inventions come from?

All of them come from a need, and an idea;
What do you think?

Every big thing comes from a lot of little things,
And anything worth while takes time to make.
What will you do?

Mother, Mother, Who Am I?

Mother, when I grow up what will I be like?
Will I be smart? Will I be tall?

Well, Lincoln freed American slaves;
He was very smart and well spoken,
And, as you know, he was also very tall.
Gandhi, though, freed an entire nation;
He had a great understanding of people,
And was not tall at all, but was instead very small.
My Dear; it's who you are inside- that's what matters!

Mother, why do people have to die?

My Dear, you are so young, you needn't worry;
But the body will eventually wear out;
Everyone someday will eventually grow old.

But what if an accident happens, what then?

Even then, the soul, the spirit, will live on.
It's that part of us that is the very essence of life;
The soul never dies- it is eternal and everlasting.

Mother, why are you always hovering over me?
Why can't I do what I want- why do you always say no?

Sweetie, it is not because I don't want you to do things;
It's not because I don't want you to have fun.
It's just because I love you, and try to look out for you;
I don't always say no- but I do want to keep you safe.

Mother, what should I do when I grow up?
Should I be one who makes things or does things?
Should I be a doctor or should I be a carpenter?

Your choices are all the things you can imagine;
All of those things about which you can do;
And all those things about which you can dream.
Find the thing that you love and make it your work.

You are so young- life can be a great adventure;
You will see many Winters, and many Springs;
And there will come some sorrow and some pain,
But you can be very happy- so much is possible.

The happy wanderer

Blue Ribbon Summer

Oh how I loved camp the Summer of '62;
The day I wandered along a wooded trail,
Happily running and singing as I went;
The dock where I'd while away the hours;
The butter and sugar sandwiches eaten.

The bonfires and the stories at evening;
Its hot embers where our dinners cooked.
The cold early morning dip in the lake;
And best of all, the blisters that I endured,
For the rowboat race that year that I won.

Dreaming

Almost Everything

Just about everything there is,
Is more than anything we can see;
Beyond this day that we know,
We can only dream- you and me.

Beyond this place where we live,
There's more than Earth and sky;
And a single glimpse of Heaven,
May just be enough for you and I.

In a moment

One Little Step, and Bam!

I thought I knew what it was to be present;
I thought I knew the world- its every form;
I never dreamed of a day quite like this one;
How fast it can change- somehow transform.

I, in the park, walking in the morning Sun;
In an instant reduced to my own surround;
Where I now stood had become everything;
Of that beyond was neither sight nor sound.

Never had I had such a strange experience;
In all the days I've walked this Earth before;
One little step from my oft trodden pathway,
And Bam! I'm through some sort of a door!

All my world suddenly in reach of my hand;
Everything outside had inside lost its place;
A leaf wafting downward my singular focus;
The big event in my little bubble of a space.

Moving still within, I found myself now out;
A somewhere beyond, and looking back in;
With the benefit now of a grand overview;
I began to think of how and where I'd been.

In the moment totally free of everything;
I could see myself now in some ways anew.
Nothing, it seems, is exactly that imagined;
I'll not be returning to that old world view.

I know I can!

Free to Be Me

I have found my heart,
I have found my faith,
For now I have found me!

I have found my soul,
I am my own great spirit,
I am awakened- I am free!

Can I Save the World

Can I save the world?
Well I can make a difference;
For this time is now my time.
Even if I've only a small part;
I can save some of the world;
This I now know- I really can!

Till morning light

In the Valley of My Dreams

When the day has given way to evening,
And evening's rest has turned to night;
When my eyelids have become too heavy,
And I've said my prayers and good-nite;
I climb into my bed and under my covers;
In the valley of dreams till morning light.

Autumn Harvest

Your quiet moments of contemplation are at times enriched with new ways to express those thoughts you've long wanted to share. Giving rise in some solemn hour to a sudden, unexpected, and brilliant illumination.

The Time of Life
(For the Autumn Time Is Harvest Time)

Every season has its own color, its own flavor- its own name;
And so it is with each and every one of us in our own time of life;
When a season of life has ended, has finally come and gone,
May that we can find some words- some way to mark its passing,
For every season in one's life has an inherent value all its own.

As the years pass the busy days of youth become more hushed;
And when those days of Summer too finally come to an end,
And the Autumn of life begins, there is time again to think;
The days, weeks, months, and years come and go more slowly;
Your longing for your lost days of Summer, that far away Spring,
Is now filled with some new thoughts- a new season has begun.

Those last days of peace and grace will come in all of our lives;
As in any other season, a Winter day too has a beauty all its own.
But the Autumn is a time to reflect, to enjoy the fruits of our work;
Indeed, as much so as any, these years are a time for celebration;
Live them to the fullest, for the Autumn time of life is harvest time.

At the end of a life's journey, no matter how short or how long,
The wayward path of a single soul must succumb to a greater course,
Its worn and weary tabernacle then finally given over to its rest.
And on the wings of a greater reality, of a vast and eternal Heaven,
Does the soul then free itself of its Earthly bonds and take flight.

Realizing that each and every life has its own enduring purpose,
Enjoy your life, learn to love, to help others- do some good things.
Will that each of us have contributed to this life what we can;
There can be no greater honor, no greater significance, than this.

What About Time

What is it that gives us our sense of time passing,
And by what markers do we measure our days?
Is it in the arrival of the daily sunrise and sunset,
Or is it in the coming and the going of the seasons?
Is it changes in the Earth, or changes in the Sun?

The Earth and the Sun appear but a small matter;
Most of what exists is more than we can imagine;
A much larger Universe lies farther out and away.
What if time is not so much of the world we know,
But is instead more a reflection of what is beyond.

What if it is not much more than a mere illusion;
What if Plato, long ago, had it all right after all;
His, "Moving and unreal reflections of eternity."
What if time is really just a perception of motion,
More a here or a there, than it is a now or a when.

So, what is the meaning of time in our own lives?
Is it about the child and the growing into adulthood?
Or is it about getting older- the coming of old-age?
It seems nearly completely beyond our experience;
Much more than a dimension of the world we know.

So much effort do we spend in its worship;
In the precise records and the calendars we make.
It is often considered to be something more linear,
But many things are found to come more in cycles,
Like birth and then death, and then there's rebirth.

One time to live may not be any better than another;
The land that our fathers gazed upon every morning,
Was not more than it is today, nor was it any less.
Nor is it the length of a lifetime that's truly important;
It's what you do with each and every day that matters.

There is something grand to be seen in every day,
In every season, and in every single time of life.
What if this day is the culmination of everything;
The stream of life- its yesterdays and its tomorrows,
Flowing into the present day, and into this moment.

Much is possible, if you, and not your ego, is in charge.
It's people that's most important, and not your things;
You will not find true happiness with someone else,
Until, within yourself, you have found the very same.

For all our deep thoughts- our heady reflections,
We try to make sense of what we'll never fully know.
How wide and deep will be found its true dimension.
But the awe of its vastness, the wonder that we feel,
The beauty that we see- these are with us always.

"It is the wounded oyster that mends its shell with pearl"- Emerson

Our Place in the Milky Way

What if this isn't reality; here, on this slowly turning Earth,
With its great oceans and mountains, its deserts and plains;
Moving along in its endless trek through the vast heavens,
Among countless galaxies and nebula- their planets and stars.

What if reality is instead out there somewhere- far beyond;
What if all that we have known is not much more than a dream;
And if this is so, will there be for us, one day, an awakening?
And, if this is so, where and when will we then find ourselves?

What then will we see as we look up into the dark starlit sky?
How will we see ourselves, and our place in time and space?
Will the vision of ancient thinkers be found any less clear?
How will we contemplate our existence? What then will we do?

A dream left alone will tend to fade and go away; a dream held true is the one that wins the day.

It Reminds Me Who I Am

There is nothing more beautiful,
Than the voice raised in song.
It calms my fears- my restless spirit;
It raises me up, and gives me rest;
It fills my soul- it inspires me;
It reminds me who I am.

The poet lays claim to a literary freedom; a license for the unbound use of words, and expression at will.

Imagine

Imagine Earth and other places,
Slowly turning, revolving, living;
The great mountains- the valleys;
Imagine the life that is all around;
Stars above, wandering, gleaming.

Think of what's real- of our place;
Just where is it we find ourselves?
Think, what is there about life?
If it's a dream, will we awaken?
And If so, what then will we do?

Dream of truth, dream of justice;
All of us breathe the same air;
Ask the world, what has it done!
Dream of things that never were,
And say, why haven't they been!

The purpose of life is the maturing of the soul- Alexander Solzhenitzyn

Of Fire and Ice

Many nights have I spent by the fire keeping warm;
Long hours of dwellings on many a pattern and form;
In hopes in some wee hour for an inspiration divine;
For some answers to questions I've long sought to find.

Outside the land sleeps, but for my one window of light;
Clear skies or no, the stars follow their trek in the night.
How they compare to a tiny atom, to flowers and trees;
I wonder what they know about their likeness to these.

Tonight I give little heed to the piling snow at my door;
My eyes on the fire, and its show of light on the floor.
A single flame is but once, and only once is the same;
Shrouded midst the blaze as the mist in an Autumn rain.

And then what of the frost and its new workings of art,
The Moon shows on my window some nights at the start.
It seems my tracings of its secrets have only just begun,
And then found and wiped clean by the new rising Sun.

Something will happen, some new and different flame;
A frosty new pattern that suddenly appears on my pane.
I search for their meaning for nights and hours on end;
That great grand-daddy of thought is not yet descend.

What do deer think, I wonder, in these woods that reside,
Stopping for a look-see, to see what there is here inside.
What do they seek, and out on a cold night in the storm,
Finding naught but just me by the fire keeping warm.

Man is born to live and not to prepare to live- Boris Pasternak

Race to the Finish

This all began with hardly a thought to what I was doing;
Not knowing what to expect, or what it was I was in for.
Before I knew it I was rounding the first curve and running;
Didn't know where I was going, but it was full speed ahead.

As I reached the second curve I could see the path in front of me,
And I gave it all I could to win that long stretch that lay before.
At the third curve I began to tire and to look back behind me;
I began to think back on the race and where it was I'd been.

As I rounded the last turn I started to put the brakes on,
For I began to get a clearer view of what there was up ahead.
I know now that I have taken this run all far too seriously,
For the finish is going to bring me back to where it all began.

A Call To All Hearts

Seems we're in for some weather,
A more severe future doth portend;
It's a change in our planet's climate,
On which we've come to depend.

The forecast calls for a climate,
More severe than before we've seen;
Changing desert, forest and coastline,
And humanity caught between.

With one great change upon us,
Another greater is at hand;
The great Atlantic Current ceasing,
Brings cold to the northern land.

The heat will still the oceans,
And cause the temperature to drop;
Heaven hath its own plan, I guess,
To make the warming stop.

Melting poles and mountain glaciers,
Are signs of what's in store;
That the climate is rapidly changing,
The voices of denial can deny no more.

It's in the geologic record,
This has happened in the past;
Before the Earth's the same again,
Many thousand years might pass.

'Tis a call to all hearts, I trumpet,
Let the quest for the future begin;
Sun, wind and atom will sustain us,
There's a challenge to meet- a world to win.

Champion of the realm, its defender,
And a good steward of the planet be.
Save it for yourself, and for your children;
Do it for you, and do it for me.

As the rain gives way to sunshine; as the summer will turn to fall; as on Earth, so it is in Heaven- the key to one is the key to all.

The Wanderer

Out into the night, the silent valley of dreams;
From the village light into the air as on a wing.
Beyond this sleepy land to a place most lucid;
To walk in the way of the ever-flowing stream.

Through field and trees- placid waters alluring;
Transcendent lunar, mist of knowing- abiding;
To look upon reflections ne'er seen, ne'er heard;
Of what has come before, and what is still to be.

In the embers of the great republic- the chosen;
The Apple falls in a summer day, cold and frozen;
From hallowed hall does a new hope then bloom;
In a thin flame, a fusion- a new dawn and spring.

To be present in the new Centauri at the arriving;
In old Tenet, in the east- sisters gleaming, rising;
In the light of heaven, to stand solitary- the elect;
In way of the high temple a great treasure to see.

Along a path to when and where- here and ever;
Dreams of what can be- where before was never;
A great and ancient heart is born and born again;
Ever the wanderer from time to place- to being.

The heart set on flame casts a great light into the darkness, it illuminates all those around. Guard this sacred fire until it blazes, for it is enough to light the world.

By the Thin Flame

The embers of knowing glow everywhere, and in every heart;
Awareness, the soul, arises from that sacred place deep within;
As a thin flame grows to become a warm and cheerful fire.

May that light which has inspired and sustained the hearts of others;
That has shown the way for those who have come before;
Now illuminate you and me!

Blessed is he who has found his work; let him ask no other blessedness
– Carlyle

My Day in the Sun

My thoughts of times long since past still linger;
Of playing in the wind in fields of golden grain;
Being in the woods when it awakens in Spring;
On a warm Summer day out walking in the rain.

They settle like the mist on my heart and mind;
A picture of Christmas, adorned in red and green,
And the breath of a cold and sunny Winter's day;
The risings and the settings of the Sun I have seen.

No better time to live has there ever before been;
And now here in this moment is my day in the Sun;
May I leave things a bit better than that I found;
To love and been loved- that's a life well done.

Whenever you happen upon an empty page, wherever you find the space, don't miss out on the opportunity to write something down.

The Cup of Love and Knowing

Knowledge is a river great and wide;
To its shores you many times have been.
Peace and wisdom, though, is a precious cup;
It is the cup of life, and it dwells within.

When you are as full of love as of knowing;
When you are as much of heart as of mind;
Your cup then is full and overflowing;
Suffering and fear, you have left behind.

Your words will attain a new sweetness,
And your voice was never before so clear.
See your cup as full as you may see it,
And your purpose and your place are here.

When that moment finally comes, when you have found out who you truly are, you are going to like what you find. You will have learned the way out of suffering; you will have won your freedom, and you will be unafraid.

On the High Forest Glen

I love to wander along the wooded mountain path:
Here are my dreams, and the hope of every Spring;
Memories of love and beauty, and of course the tears,
Lie still amid the Autumn leaves and Winter snow.

It's a sort of monument I've made to myself I suppose;
I want to call it a life of knowledge and experience,
All crafted by me, one carefully cut stone at a time;
But my heart tells me there's more to it than that.

Lately I've found a clearing along my oft trodden way;
A something more than my thinking can explain.
It is of no time or place, and it teaches above our days;
As the Sun shines the same on every village and house.

Above wanting, birth and death, is a higher calling;
It is our awareness that gives what we know meaning;
It presents an ever broadening horizon, it has no limit;
When I find my compass it's in the reflection of its light.

Tonight I look out upon a vast and dark and starry sky;
In the green of Summer, I stand on a high forest glen;
There's no words- it's just me, face-to-face with heaven;
I stretch forth my hand and I touch the brightest star.

CPSIA information can be obtained
at www.ICGtesting.com
Printed in the USA
LVHW080738080621
689597LV00009B/614